if you find the BUDDHA

if you find the BUDDHA

Photographs by Jesse Kalisher
Foreword by Jeff Greenwald

CHRONICLE BOOKS
SAN FRANCISCO

Library of Congress Cataloging-in-Publication Data available.

ISBN 0-8118-4814-0

Manufactured in China

Designed by Celery Design Collaborative

Distributed in Canada by Raincoast Books
9050 Shaughnessy Street
Vancouver, British Columbia V6P 6E5

10 9 8 7 6 5 4 3 2 1

Chronicle Books LLC
85 Second Street
San Francisco, California 94105
www.chroniclebooks.com

for Helen:

> You are my muse. Your love, your talent,
> and your never-ending belief in me made
> this book possible. I am, as always, madly
> in love with you.

Foreword

Some time ago, walking down a street in Istanbul, I came upon a riveting sight. It was the Turkish version of a shoeshine stand: a gleaming, multilevel platform of polished brass, like something right out of *The Time Machine*. The base of the stand was decorated with images in ornate gold frames. Two of them caught my eye: a portrait of the Virgin Mary and, beside her, a luscious pinup of Marilyn Monroe. The dissonance was shocking—like seeing the pope pulling from a hip flask.

It occurred to me, then, how *inhibiting* religious figures can be. Stumbling upon them, in images or in the flesh, can create an immediate sense of awkwardness, the same gnawing self-consciousness one feels when driving alongside a patrol car.

A Buddha image, on the other hand, never feels intrusive. Its appearance may seem ironic if one identifies him merely as the antithesis of the material world. But for many, especially of course throughout Asia, he's a far more complex symbol. The Buddha doesn't simply represent a non-grasping state of mind; he reminds us that everything we're experiencing, right here and right now, is exactly as it must be—and utterly transitory. The only way to avoid suffering (i.e., wishing things had been better in the past, or that they will be better in the future) is to inhabit the present moment with our entire being—whether we're caught in traffic, running a bank, or spinning a hula hoop.

The most ironic thing about Buddha images is that they exist at all. Buddha himself forbade any likenesses of him—and for half a millennium his directive was honored. His presence was symbolized not by the image we know today but by evocative symbols. These included the lotus (which is rooted in muck but blossoms into purity), the eight-spoke wheel (a reminder of the Eightfold Path to liberation), and the Bodhi tree (a *ficus religiosa,* which sheltered the meditating Buddha).

As the centuries passed, though, a couple of things happened. First, traffic along the Silk Road brought artists and techniques from the Greco-Roman world to the Indian subcontinent—specifically to Gandhara, in what is now northern Pakistan. The legendary Buddha was an irresistible subject. Most Asian art collections have examples of these third- and fourth-century Buddhas. Tall, imposing, and sporting neat moustaches, they look more like Greek matinee idols than Nepal-born sages.

The reason these images endured is that Buddha's followers began to get restless. It's no wonder; anyone who has visited the Indian subcontinent is aware of how seductive her gods and goddesses can be. Take Laxmi, with her opened hands dripping gold coins, or Shiva, with the drum of creation in one hand and flames of destruction in the other. And who can resist elephant-headed Ganesha, Remover of Obstacles, gesturing with one hand while the other palms his favorite snack?

A wheel, or even a tree, has nothing on these guys. If Buddhism wanted to stay on the map, it had to offer its followers an image they could identify with.

On one hand, this was a mistake—the first step toward turning Buddha into a god, and Buddhahood into a divine state, beyond the reach of humans. I think Buddha himself would have been perturbed (as much as Buddha was ever perturbed) by the sight of people praying to his image; idol worship was one of the bad habits he was trying to quell in ancient India. Not only that, treating Buddha as a god undermines his whole achievement. The most encouraging thing about Buddhism (which brims with tough-love teachings) is that Siddhartha Gautama, the historical Buddha, was *not* a god. He was a human being—a guy who worked hard, meditated with conviction, and transcended the snares of desire and attachment.

On the other hand, he's a great visual. I mean, here's a guy sitting down, eyes half-closed, in a state of total relaxed awareness. In one traditional *mudra* his fingers are entwined, teaching; in another, he's touching the Earth, inviting the planet itself to witness his awakening. His face, half-smiling, has the hypnotic effect of a cloudscape. It's virtually impossible to look at a Buddha for any length of time (including those fat, laughing Buddhas, who actually depict the Zen beggar-monk Hotei) without feeling a sense of calm and well-being.

That's certainly the feeling that arises from Jesse Kalisher's photographs. As with a lover—or a close relative, or good friend—meeting the Buddha is always a welcome surprise. Like those familiar faces, it snaps us back to what's truly important: the joy of community, the value of kindness, and the benefits of being focused and engaged, whatever our enterprise.

These are principles we can stand to be reminded of, over and over again, as we navigate this baffling human realm. And binding them together is a central mystery, revealed to very few—but known with absolute clarity by the Buddha. It's the mystery of why our conduct in this world matters, and what role—if any—we are meant to fill in the cosmos.

This, too, is what the Buddha represents: the common denominator of our collective awareness, in all its riotous forms. That's why he's as appropriate around the neck of a Thai soldier as he is on a golf course; as correct as a decorative candle, with a wick coming out of his head, as in a sun-washed temple.

Every image in this book provokes a different response—but all potentially bring us to the same understanding. Maybe that's why my personal favorite is the photograph of the little girl with the hula hoop. It reminds me of a teaching delivered to me in a fortune cookie, following a dish called Buddha's Delight:

We dance in a circle and suppose
The truth sits in the center, and knows.

—Jeff Greenwald
Colombo, Sri Lanka

Introduction: *the* Unexpected Buddha

by Jesse Kalisher

On the same spot I sit today
Others came, in ages past, to sit.
One thousand years, still others will come.
Who is the singer, and who is the listener?
—Nguyen Cong Tru

While working on this book during one very hot and wet day in Bangkok, I met an intriguing monk at a famous temple called Wat Pho. The monk's name was Panom, and he looked no more than twenty-five years old, with clean skin that covered a gentle, round face. Despite his curiosity about my project, Pat Panom had reservations about helping me. Tourists had recently been arrested for disrespecting a Thai Buddha; they had climbed atop it to pose for a snap-shot, and Pat Panom was concerned that, while he could prevent me from climbing on any statues, he had no idea how I would use my images of Buddha. I assured Pat Panom that my intent with this book was honorable and, at his request, handwrote and signed my commitment to respect Buddha and Bud-dhism with my photographs.

Having overcome his initial reservations, Pat Panom guided me through the vast temple grounds and regaled me with stories about the grand temple, about the great reclining Buddha it contained, and about the giant that great reclining Buddha had slain. When I asked him, Pat Panom talked easily about the arc of his own life and about the choice he soon faced: whether to remain a monk or to become a civilian, which would require him to spend a mandatory three years in the military.

When he wasn't sharing stories about Buddha or about himself, Pat Panom asked about my thoughts on religion, on God, on the teachings of Buddha, and on some of the nuances of the English language. "What does it mean: 'revere'?" he asked me. "Is it the same as worship?"

"No," I told him. I explained that one might revere a king but worship a god.

One reason Pat Panom was so helpful to me was that he embraced this book's concept. "People should know Buddha," he said. "Not just statues, but everywhere." And so he gave me unrestricted access to the Wat Pho compound, long before the official open hours when the tour buses began lining up at the front gate. He took me to see a group of chanting monks. He took me to his private quarters. And he took me to the foot of a bodhi tree, the very type of tree that Buddha sat under when he ascended to his state of ultimate enlightenment.

At the foot of this particular tree at Wat Pho (as at the foot of many bodhi trees in Thailand) were scattered hundreds of medallion-sized Buddhas. Pat Panom excitedly explained how it was that those Buddha medallions came to be there. When people have a string of bad luck in their lives, he told me, they believe they can turn it around by placing a small Buddha at the foot of a bodhi tree.

"Nobody understands why the Buddha is here at this tree," Pat Panom lamented, referring, of course, to Western tourists. To this day, I don't understand why this was as important to him as it was. But it *was* important to him, and he asked me several times, emphatically, to promise to explain here why worshippers place Buddha medallions at the foot of a bodhi tree.

So I promised.

"Tell them," he repeated, "it is to change bad luck."

Our conversation meandered and eventually Pat Panom asked me how it is that I came to be a photographer. Actually, I have always been a photographer. My father is a celebrated photographer, and, thanks to him, I had my first camera by the time I could walk. A darkroom soon followed. As a result, I experimented with photography from my earliest years through high school. Once in college, however, the camera and I parted ways; photography quickly became a memory, a ghost that moved around in my mind, still a part of me but one that never quite managed to materialize.

"But you are a photographer," Pat Panom pointed out.

"Yes, I am," I smiled. And then I shared with Pat Panom the story of how I came to be freed from the traditional shackles of a desk, paycheck, and two-week vacation.

When I think about it, everything hinges on a time when I thought a lot about the power of belief. When I was seven years old, for instance, I wondered if I leaped from my third-story apartment window would I then, like Superman, soar above Metropolis, if only I believed strongly enough in my ability to fly.

Fortunately, sanity set in before I put this question to the ultimate test. Still, I formed a strong attachment to this idea of belief, and it became part of a two-part promise I made to myself at a young age: that I would always consider life an adventure and that, within reason, I would believe myself capable of doing just about anything.

As an eight-year-old who rode a Manhattan public bus to school by myself, living up to this ideal was as simple as challenging myself to befriend the bus driver. Each morning, I stepped onto the number 4 bus, which took me on a forty-five-minute journey to my Upper Eastside grammar school. I got on the same bus every day, the 7:58, so I could ride with the same driver, a gentle man named Frank with a long face and a big laugh. Sure enough, Frank and I became pals. And while I wasn't allowed to actually touch the money (this was back in 1970, when New York City bus drivers still made change for passengers), Frank let me run the manual drop bar on the coin-collection machine.

I loved that.

Of course, confidence didn't always come easily over the years, and, as one would expect, it wasn't the answer to all of life's challenges. Of my many setbacks, the guitar comes to mind; also the high school football team. And, certainly, girls. If only I had known about the power of placing Buddhas at the foot of a bodhi tree back in high school . . . but then, I doubt I could have found a bodhi tree in Manhattan.

As I grew older, I refined my philosophy. Failure was acceptable, I reasoned. Not trying, however— certainly not trying due to lack of faith in myself— was not. What I wanted was simple: I wanted to explore the edges of my comfort zone. I didn't need to climb Everest, compete in a triathlon, or bicycle from one tip of Africa to the other. But what I did need to do was reject complacency, to move away from the expected path of my life.

I succeeded in my quest for a short time after

college; there was a stint working at a ski resort, for example. But then student loans needed to be repaid. And the fear of floundering for too long began to take over. So I moved back to New York and got a job. And a television set.

That's when I lost a decade of my life.

In the midst of this lost decade, in an effort to change my life, I moved from an advertising job in New York to an advertising job in San Francisco. I began cycling to work and eventually unplugged my television set. I thought these changes would be enough to save my life. I was wrong.

I never saw it coming, but I hit an emotional wall. A day came when I locked the door to my office, closed my blinds, forwarded my phone to my narcoleptic secretary, fell to the floor, and cried. Quite simply, I broke down.

Sitting on the floor inside my office, I took in my surroundings and moaned. I moaned because I suddenly saw my life as being restricted to a series of small boxes. I thought in terms of physical boxes: my apartment, my car, my office, and so on. Of course there were metaphysical boxes restricting me as well, ones that would become obvious to me over time. Crying on the floor of my office, I remembered the long-forgotten promise I'd made to myself as a child, a promise about the power of adventure and belief.

Pat Panom might have said that I needed to change my luck.

Before long, I pulled myself off the floor and, with equal measures of desperation and confidence, wrote my letter of resignation.

This was the beginning of my rehabilitation.

Nine months later, I boarded a flight to Hanoi. It was 1996, just six months after we normalized relations with Vietnam. This was only my second trip outside of America, and it was my first trip to a developing nation. I found Vietnam, and Hanoi in particular, remarkable. In Hanoi, for instance, a city in which no building could stand taller than Ho Chi Minh's mausoleum, the roads were filled with bicycles, mopeds, and only the occasional car. There were no traffic lights, which meant that crossing the street became an exercise in controlled chaos. For a boy who grew up jaywalking in Manhattan, I was fascinated to find that I could fly halfway around the world to this underdeveloped city and suddenly find myself challenged in something as basic as crossing the street.

On my second day in Vietnam, I went for a stroll just as the sun broke over the horizon—well before the morning rush of two-wheeled vehicles. To my surprise, I saw children everywhere. A group of them had parked their bicycles on either side of the street and had strung nets between them. Over those nets, they played badminton.

Somewhere in the world, someone had just placed a Buddha medallion at the base of a bodhi tree with me in mind—because as I watched ten- and twelve-year-olds play in the middle of Hanoi's streets, I felt the enormity of a powerful idea: that there was an entire planet waiting to be discovered. And I became determined to see as much of that planet as possible. These handful of Vietnamese children changed my view of the world. And, in the process, they changed me.

Then something truly brilliant happened. It was there, as I stood in front of these kids playing badminton, that I rediscovered my love affair with the camera.

Before leaving for Vietnam, I had bought an inexpensive point-and-shoot camera with the idea that I would capture a few casual snapshots. But when I brought that camera to my eye and looked at those kids playing badminton, I had an epiphany.

Where I thought I would see a snapshot, I saw instead a photograph. Where I expected to record a memory, I found meaning. Where I anticipated a sense of frivolity, I was taken over instead by a wave of overwhelming emotion. Indeed, through that tiny lens I found peace—and reality. That's when I knew I had found my voice.

Having the opportunity to create this book took me back to Asia for the fourth time and launched me on another adventure of the exact kind I'd pledged to seek out as a child; an adventure that pushed my boundaries and challenged me to believe in myself. This is the adventure that brought me back to Bangkok, to Wat Pho, and ultimately to Pat Panom.

As Pat Panom and I walked through the temple grounds and discussed everything from photography and global politics to his upcoming philosophy dissertation, Pat Panom invariably steered the conversation back to this one idea: the power of placing a Buddha at the base of a bodhi tree.

I asked him if it works—if placing a small Buddha at the base of a tree can actually change one's luck.

Pat Panom smiled and would not answer. "People believe," he said finally. "Perhaps that is enough."

Plates

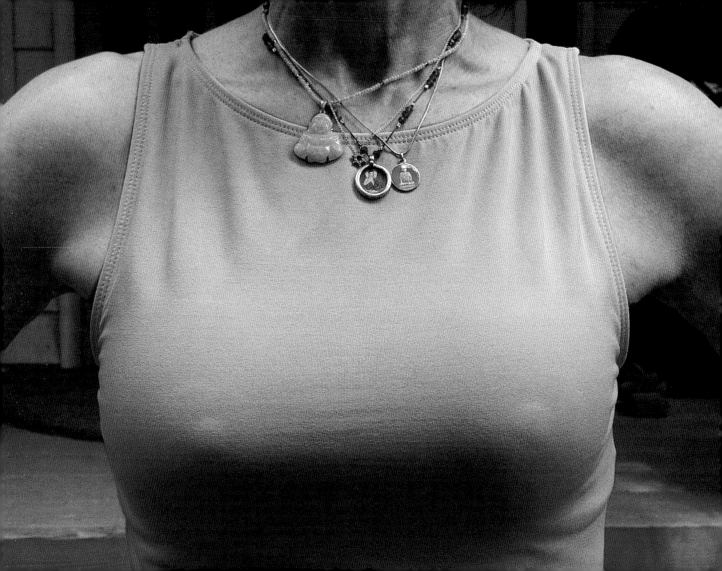

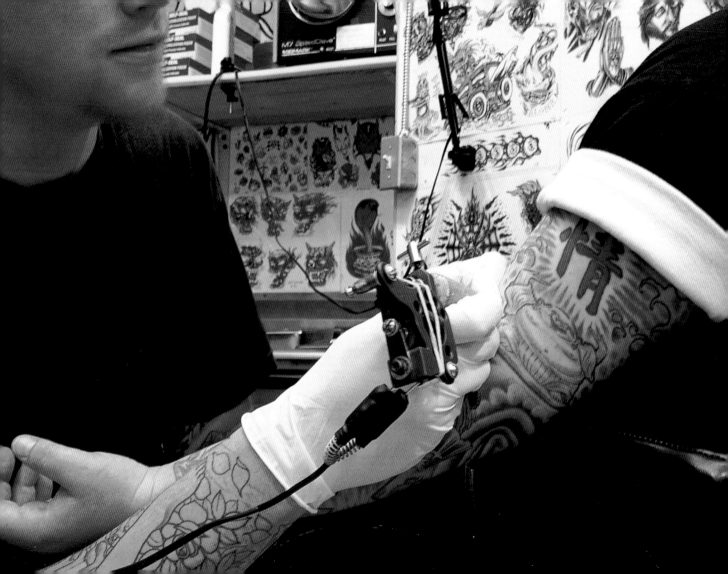

buddha-bar

By Claude Challe

disc
ONE
Buddha's
Party

Aprés
les succès des
BAINS DOUCHES,
LOVER-DOSE et
FLYING CARPET,
voici la nouvelle compilation
inclus
SHAFT
by MALIK

BUDDHA BAR

PU 131

a child was born
and sad ly I love ed the little baby boy
my sun flew round the wing ed sky
and time cried for his silent song
he glow s inside my cry ing heart
where light is dark and day is night

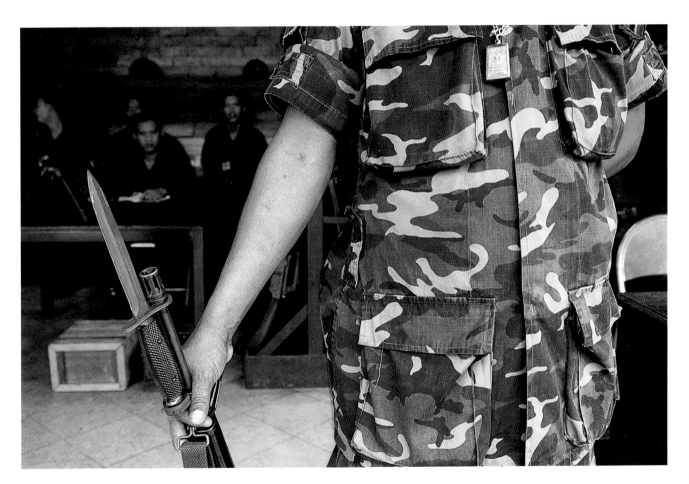